To Noreen,
Merry Christmas!,
David Blyl

The First Act of Creation

The First Act of Creation

On the Way to Emmanuel

David Michael Belczyk

RESOURCE *Publications* · Eugene, Oregon

Resource Publications
An Imprint of Wipf and Stock Publishers
199 W. 8th Ave., Suite 3
Eugene, OR 97401

www.wipfandstock.com
www.davidbelczyk.com

PAPERBACK ISBN: 978-1-7252-8775-4
HARDCOVER ISBN: 978-1-7252-8776-1
EBOOK ISBN: 978-1-7252-8777-8

Manufactured in the U.S.A. 10/07/20

Ecclesiastical Permission

Nihil Obstat: A. J. Schrenk, Censor Deputatus
Imprimatur: +David A. Zubik, Bishop of Pittsburgh
August 12, 2020

Ecclesiastical permission is a declaration that a work is considered to be free
from doctrinal or moral error. It is not implied that those who have granted the
same agree with the contents, opinions or statements expressed.

Profits from the sale of this book support Holy Family Hospital in the Holy Land, enabling works of mercy and peace throughout the region. In our unity that flows from the Incarnation, when caring for the sick, feeding the hungry, clothing the naked, inviting the stranger, we have done the same to Christ Himself, (Matthew 25:35–40).

CONTENTS

PREFACE

The First Act of Creation is an Advent devotional comprised of fourteen lyric and contemplative "Stations," modeled after the familiar Lenten Stations of the Cross. These Advent Stations, however, reflect on the Incarnation and the long-awaited revelation of the Messiah. Instead of walking the path to Calvary, these Advent Stations trace a path through salvation history. They approach the Nativity and Christ's identity via the meaning of the Incarnation, which is the mystery of our own existence.

These Advent Stations are meant for communal and individual prayer, reflection, and teaching related to Advent. Like Lenten Stations of the Cross, they can be led by a pastor, religious, or lay person, with the italicized stanzas read by the congregation. They can serve as explorations of topics for small groups, catechumens, and religion classes. They can be contemplated alone, with the italics representing creation's dialogue with the Creator (a dialogue joined, at the station of the Visitation, by the voice of the Church proclaiming the Gospel).

These Stations seek to join the theological depth of the Incarnation with familiar events of the Christmas story, as God's divine plan takes root in our humanness. They reflect on the promise of a Messiah, a wait during which our nature in God's image labors for God's fruitfulness. They draw upon the prophets, who glimpsed the eternal truth of oneness with Christ's humanity not only in the Nativity but in Christ's triumphant return and the Resurrection of the Body.

The Stations begin with Genesis, the start of the Christmas story, when God creates that which He has willed to be and is, to begin the revelation of this glory to His creation. God makes the flesh, which will reveal Him in the fullness of time, and places His temple within the larger tabernacle of the world, to enshrine us in the beauty and mystery of nature. The Stations end with the Holy Family returning from their flight to Egypt, when Christ retraces the ancient trail of the Exodus in prefiguration of His salvific mission and identity. The Eucharist features throughout as our realization of the Incarnation, because in the Eucharist we are, now, physically one with the Incarnate flesh and thus paradise.

I had the idea for these Advent Stations on Epiphany and first drafted them during Lent 2013. They are the companion to *The Final Act of Creation*, a lyric Stations of the Cross that I wrote during Lent 2011. The *First Act* is the theological fulfillment and completion of the *Final Act*, because the completion of our creation directs us to the reason for our creation, as Christ's Passion is a fulfillment of Christ's identity. And Christ's identity is shared with us because we are Children of God.

We may find comfort in the Passion because we know our own suffering—and we know what it is like to beg for the Resurrection when gripped by our mortality and our failures. The Passion is the supreme stroke of creation in which even death, and thus all, is subjected and transformed according to God's loving will. But that accomplishment follows after God has already loved us, and chosen us, and chosen the Passion. We should see in ourselves all that God has ordained us to be from the beginning. A meaning of suffering evinces a meaning of life. The beauty of the Passion expresses the beauty of existence. The *First Act* explores the beauty of what it means to be human. What it means to be that which God is become. We are each of us the eternal living temples of the eternal God.

The first and final truth is that God lives. God is life. All things that exist have their life in God. And all life is good. As I did with the *Final Act*, I write again to sanctify my art, because art is nothing unless it is life. Creators, overcome with the need for and cross of fruitfulness, can forget that we are here to love and be loved, that God is sufficient, that He will draw out of us pilgrims that which is according to His will, contrary to temporal notions of art, creation, labor, and self.

Contemplating the Incarnation leads to astounding and thrilling conclusions about what it means to be human. The Incarnation reveals that we, though creatures, are one with God. Through the identity of Christ, we are God's own children. And God dwells in all people, in the flesh that He has made His temple. This truth has radical implications for how we live. It governs how we love others as well as ourselves—love as God has loved us. It gives us unapproachable and unspeakable hope. It is miraculous that we may have such hope, and yet it is a hope that we must have and must maintain. If we receive God in our temples, He unfolds for us the sublime joy of creation and His creative being, and fills us with the endless life that He is.

Contemplating the Incarnation also reveals life's meaning and its beauty. The Incarnation is truly the First of our life, because Christ's humanity is eternal with Him. Fully God and fully human, without the mixing or lessening of either nature, Christ takes up and carries the flesh into eternal reality, through the Resurrection, as intended from the beginning. Because of Christ, both creation and the Resurrection are within the temples of our flesh. The Kingdom of Heaven itself is within us, as Christ teaches. The Incarnation and the Resurrection are the same living mystery, as our eternal life and salvation were accomplished in God's will for our oneness in Christ. The Incarnation reveals how and why the Passion restores humanity to God's paradisal flesh from creation's beginning. The Passion returns us to the identity for which God made us.

We know our own life fully when we see the majesty of the Incarnation. The Incarnation and the Passion are not only a response to sin. That singular view would suggest that sin can compel God, and it would strip the generative beauty of the Incarnation that flows from God's timelessness. Rather, the whole cause of creation must be the love that God is, and the divine desire for love and unity with a creation capable of love in return—a desire so great as to be merciful. The Incarnation is not only something that had to happen on Christ's way to Calvary. Rather we are here for God's will to be Incarnate, because of God's love and His desire to love us. The Incarnation is the truth of God that is the meaning for our life. This is consistent with the age-old formula that the purpose of life is to know, love, and serve God, because the paradise of God is both the source and direction of life. It is also consistent with a newer formulation that has been used with children: that God made us because He thought we would like it. He makes Himself our own pinnacle. The Incarnation allows us to understand the proclamation of St. Irenaeus that the glory of God is man fully alive—following the model of Christ and His conquering love, our very flesh is a part of the eternal glory of God's creative will.

Because Christ is the First Fruits, the Alpha, the Love of the beginning, the new Adam, the Word through which all things are made, He is the reason for the existence of humanity, and the font of all existence. We are made in the image of God, not only in our will and our love and our own creating, but also because of God's will that we be one and He be human. This oneness in the flesh is an eternal reality of God's creative will and of the Word. It is not a oneness in which we are God or rival God—beautifully, God concedes none of His divinity and we concede none of our identity—but yet the majesty of being children of God is revealed, as is the majesty of the Spirit that indwells us, in a fulfillment that eye has not seen and ear has not heard, as Christ says. Participation in the life of God is unimaginably deep and vibrant. Athanasius taught that it divinizes us, saying "the Son of God became man that we might become God." Humanity is created in time, and in time the Word became flesh and dwelt among us. But at the same time God's plan of incarnation was before our creation and part of the creative act. Being made in the image of God means, in part, being made in the image of the Incarnate Christ, who is God and human forevermore.

As we are in the image of God, God is present to us as human, and our oneness in God's creative love is complete. Christ humbled Himself to become human, but humanity exists in the glory of what flesh Christ, in His identity, willed to become. That is why the creation of humanity is the start of the Christmas story, when God brings us to life in the flesh, to prepare us, within the setting of human time, for the revelation of I Am in the person of Christ. And in Christ, the endless Love of the Passion points finally to this meaning of our creation.

God made us in love, because He first willed in His love to be one creatively and salvifically with His creation. We exist for the purpose of the Incarnation. The Incarnation is the first act of creation. I direct the reader to the writings of Karl Rahner on the Incarnation as the reason for existence, which served as the inspiration for this undertaking.

In Pope Francis's "The Name of God is Mercy," we encounter the story about a woman who says, "the world would not exist without mercy." We see this truth in the Incarnation. Without mercy there would not be the redemptive identity of Christ, there would not be the creation of an imperfect being capable of love for the purpose of the Incarnation, there would not be then free will or the fall. God in mercy made us the fullness of creation that is incarnate. We are saved for God to be incarnate, so, without mercy, we would not be. The purpose of the world would not be.

Pope Benedict XVI also explores the eternalness of the Incarnation throughout the "Jesus of Nazareth" infancy narratives. Within the name of Jesus is the name of the Tetragrammaton, where God reveals Himself as what is. This name is expanded, consistent with Jesus' identity, into God Saves. At the annunciation, Mary is "overshadowed" by the Holy Spirit, as the overshadowing of the ancient temple where God's presence is both known and concealed in the column of cloud, as God is in a tiny cell in the Ark of the Virgin. This perpetual consistency might even be understood, as described by Michael O'Brien in "Father Elijah," not only as prefigurement but more so as differing perspectives, in time, of the same event or reality.

Our oneness with God is perpetual, first in the perpetual person of Christ who is fully God and fully human. Also it is perpetual in the Church, forever Christ's body. Communally the Church lives forever Christ's sacrament, and it is made of our lives and our bodies, which are forever the temples in which God lives and dwells. Moreover, this oneness is complete in the Eucharist, where we commune even physically with the true flesh, the resurrected body, the flesh in paradise before the exile, the command of the Word, the reason for life.

Similarly, because Christ is both Alpha and Omega, beginning and end, first and last, residing in the Incarnation is the promise of His return. It is hard to prepare for the end of time because of an attachment to the world that we know. So much striving is entwined with mortal ending. This attachment stems from thinking too little of ourselves, not too much. But the Incarnation reveals what it means to be fully human in the timeless paradise of God. Moreover, the Incarnation reveals that what we do to those around us is also what we do to Christ, because of the oneness of our humanity and because of the indwelling of the Spirit and the entire Kingdom of God. As Camus writes in "The Fall," the great secret of the last judgment is that it happens every day.

Proceeds from this book support the Church's mission work by funding care for mothers and babies at the Holy Family Hospital in Bethlehem (just a short walk from the birthplace of Christ) and helping to make possible life-saving works of mercy. It is my hope that the reader will feel solidarity with the needy whom this book supports, those in whom Christ dwells, and this solidarity will add meaning to these Stations. As Pope Francis said in an audience during Advent 2013: by trusting us with one another and with our own humanity, Christ trusts us with Himself, as he trusted us with His own vulnerable infant body. Whatsoever we do to the least among us we do to Him.

So these Stations are called "First," because the Incarnation is the mystery of our existence and the start of our identity and humanity. Their companion is called "Final" because, in the Passion and Resurrection, Christ restores and completes humanity, making us as we were intended from the beginning, ready to face the end of time. The Passion is how God reconciles our salvific destiny with our free will that is the necessary component of our ability to love. The Passion is the reality of God's endless love that is our genesis. But to live in love, the Incarnation reveals who we are and why we are here. Between the "First" and the "Final" is the life of our Messiah, all beauty, all promise, all living—all our life and the joy of creation and the very few things that we may hope to call selfless.

DAVID MICHAEL BELCZYK
Pittsburgh
December 2018

We adore You, O Christ,
And we praise You,

By Your Holy Incarnation
You give us Life.

GENESIS

In the beginning is the Word,
and the Word is with God, and the Word is God.
All things come to be through Him;
without Him nothing comes to be.
What comes to be through Him is life,
and this life is our light.

The light shines in the darkness,
and the darkness cannot comprehend it.
Enlightening truth comes into the world.
He is in the world; the world lives in Him.
He is in the flesh that is His own,
before the world knew Him.

My Word pours forth,
before the earth, before depths,
or springs of water or mountains.
When I established the heavens
and made the vault over the face of the deep.

The Word was His delight day by day—
playing before the Father like a child,
delighting in humanity.

With my Word, I made light
and separated it from dark.
I made the sky.
With my Word, I gathered the waters
and raised up fertile land that gives fruit.
I made the sun and moon and stars,
the depth of time, the mystery of place.
With my Word, I made every bird
and all creatures in the teeming waters.
I made the land animals,
powerful beast and fragile victim.

All that I have made is good.
Lift up your eyes and see who has created.
The earth and its fullness are mine.
With my Word I make knowledge of myself.

You will me to know you,
to touch you, to receive you:
I Am the Word and the command of creation.
I Am love.

I love you.
In the beginning I made you
in my divine image of love.
Male and Female I created you.
I Am creating you because I love you.
And I Am creating you to love you.
I give you my abundant life that is.

My Word knit you in the womb.
Before I formed you I knew you.
Before you were born I dedicated you.
In the tabernacle of creation's awe,
all your beauty and all your time
spill from my will to love.

You did not choose me, but I choose you.
I choose you in my Word,
to be holy and unblemished.
I loved you before the foundation of the world,
as the Father loves the Son.
I choose my love and its destiny.

For the glory of my love, I make you,
and make you my own temple,
and make my temple eternal.
I enshrine you in my resplendent glory.
I bring the world forth from the formless abyss.
And give it to you.

You have called me for your victory of life.
You made me your covenant,
a light to open the eyes of the blind,
to bring prisoners from confinement,
and from the dungeon those who live in darkness.
You clothed me with salvation
and wrapped me in your justice,
a bride alight with jewels,
a groom adorned.

Then I breathed in your lungs of clay.
I extended my hands
and put my Word in your mouth.
I set you over nations and kingdoms,
to root up and tear down,
to destroy, to build and plant.

Nothing separates us; I walk with you in the garden.
See me Incarnate before you.

THE PROMISE OF A SAVIOR

I love you.
I did not create you to destroy you
but to call you to me.
I Am compassionate to all my works.

I promise myself to you.
I give you my Word
when I breathe in your lungs of clay.
To be one with you
I made the universe and gave you my life.
I raise up your temple from nothing.
Believe in me.
I Am faithful to my creation.

I know your exile.
I knew it before I fashioned you from its dust.
It lives in the name of our oneness
and in the One I send.
I knew how I would labor
to exult your will with love.

It is for the glory of your love that you save me.
God takes on His creation
as creation reflects its God.

So I made my promise and said:
I will put enmity between you and the Woman
and between your offspring and hers.
He will strike at your head
while you strike at his heel.

In my exile you accomplish my creation
by the death I have caused in life,
when you subjugate all,
bending even death to your saving will.
This is the fidelity of the Word,
His identity since I am willed in His image.
The fall was before Him
when He was the Word before the fall.

Woman, you suffer all your life
the pain of labor.
You are in the image of God.
The Word suffers in exile to create you.

Man, you labor to bring fruit
from the dirt from which you are taken
and shall return.
You are in the image of God,
who labors now to bring creation to fulfillment.

And all creation groans in labor pains.
By many paths searching for God,
finding the relic of eternal promise in the heart
and calling out, *Messiah,*
as the voice of one crying out in the wilderness.
The raw and wild clay and the work of my hands,
they know their destiny and their need.
It must be I who saves them.

I, unbelieving flesh, cry out:
Father our redeemer, you are named forever.
O that you would rend the heavens
and come down, mountains quaking before you.
We have withered like leaves,
and our guilt carries us away in the wind.
If you take away our breath, we perish
and return to the dust.
Send forth your Spirit and we are created,
and you renew the face of the earth.

I Am coming
to renew your flesh with the beginning,
to create a new heaven and a new earth.
I Am coming in glory and submission
to finish in revelation what I began in mystery,
to be complete with you, even in death.
I Am coming now, and I Am coming always.
I Am with you even to the end of time.

You have seen me, and you will see me.
Come to me all who labor and are burdened,
and I will give you rest.

Prophets prepare the way.
Bring water from dry rocks, open seas,
bring down bread from heaven.
I never leave you, in my bread or in my body.
I touch burning embers of the Word to your lips
afire with the Spirit that will descend.
I give the law in pure and unconsuming fire
upon my mountain,
to keep the truth of God before your eyes
while you bear the wait for the fullness of time.

The night is advanced; the day is at hand.
The Virgin shall conceive and bear a son,
and you shall call Him Emmanuel.
Many will come to my mountain,
and I will bind up their wounds.
Wait patiently.
You do not know when Messiah is coming.
The end comes like a thief in the night.

Father forever, I cry out weak with wait:
I will not be quiet
until your vindication shines like dawn,
and victory like a burning torch.
Creation will be called a new name
pronounced by your Word.
We shall be a glorious crown in your hand.

My creation, I delight in you
as a groom rejoices in his bride.
My eternal kingship blossoms with the Spirit
and the gifts of the Spirit.

I judge the poor with justice.
My breath fills the void,
destroys the void,
and makes it teem with life.
I fill the earth with knowledge of God
as water covers the sea.

The infant will play unharmed with the serpent.
And into the peace of paradise
a little child shall lead them.

THE IMMACULATE CONCEPTION

The afflicted, the needy
seek water in vain,
their tongues parched with thirst.
I answer them.
I do not forsake them.
I open streams of paradise in the desert.

O my precious creation,
You have enslaved yourselves to the now.
You have enslaved yourselves to yesterday
and tomorrow.

But you will see your splendor raised,
the jewel you are in the crown of my creation,
when you see who I Am.
I uplift you
to love you.
See how nothing is more beautiful
than an innocent child.

I Am Who Is creating me,
who has always been creating me,
you have given yourself to me,
to finish in flesh what you began in clay.

Woman, you temple
that is the Son's nature,
I make you pure because He is pure.
He is your unblemished atonement.
He is the flesh of fulfillment.
The paradise of the beginning.

I free you because He is free
and because it is my will.
Sin has no power over me.
I free you from your own creation,
from your own inheritance.

But I do not take away your humanness
any more than I could take away myself.
Your flesh is from the beginning for Him,
but your will is forever your own.
And we shall see its glory.

Precious Mother,
Full of Grace,
through you all have me
though not all have your freedom yet.
In a broken world sin remains.

I do not return you to the garden
for the pain of another exile.
The world would still cry for the Savior.
The flesh would still wait for our oneness.
I make you the garden.

O necessary sin of Adam!
O happy fault that earned so glorious a Redeemer!

The desert will exult and bloom
and rejoice in song.
Then I will see the splendor of God.
Strengthen those who are weak or frightened
so they may see the image in their flesh.

With this flesh
He opens
eyes of the blind and ears of the deaf.
And the lame leap and the mute speak.
The confused mind clears.
The oppressed have justice.

With this flesh
The hungry are fed.
The brokenhearted are healed.
Captives are set free.

Rivers burst forth in the desert,
and we are crowned with beginnings.

BETROTHAL TO JOSEPH

In the beginning, Man,
I joined you with this Woman
to preserve
God in His temple.

You have been calling to your pure one
from the beginning:
Arise my beloved,
My dove, my beautiful one, and come.

The winter is past.
The storms are over and gone.
Flowers appear in the fields.
The vines in bloom give their fragrance.
The tree bears fruit,
and the dove sings.

O my dove in the clefts of the rock,
in the secret recesses of the cliff.
Let me see you.
Let me hear your voice.
Your voice is sweet, and you are lovely.

Receive this dove
as Noah who saw the flood was over,
as my Church is lifted on the flood waters.
Now my Church is become your dove.
Love her as I have loved
the ascending dove of the flesh.

Father,
bring all life to your living body.
Raise up Children of God.
God who dwells in us,
raise all life to your promise.
Father the Church.

Holy Family,
Trinity, as one, bring life from nothing.
That God may be complete in His humanity,
humanity may know the creation of God.

Let your children come to me.
All your children are my own;
all life belongs to me.
Together, creator, we increase the life that I Am.

I authored life for my love,
and I deliver to you this temple
that I have sanctified,
this dove that comes to me
transfigured upon soaring wings.

The Word of the divine
comes to your humble ears, Man,
to speak to you
the sweetest secrets of your longing heart,
to show you
the things you cannot understand you want,
when all you know is your thirst.

In your first dream the divine will come to you,
when you find the child of the Holy Spirit:
love your wife as I love my Church,
to return to God the splendor of the given Word.
Love her innocence without blemish.

Behold the Virgin shall bear a son
and we shall call him Emmanuel.

You are to name Him Jesus,
because He will save people from their sins.

Save me, Father, with your fatherhood.
To heal my selfishness
give me the mystery of creation.
Pour your Holy Spirit into the temple
you have purified.
I carry your Incarnation to the hungry world.
You married my hunger with your promise.

I trust in the Father's redemption.
His praise is ever in my mouth.
My soul glories in the Lord and in His dove.
I look to Him, I Am radiant with joy.

THE ANNUNCIATION

Rejoice, Full of Grace!
The Lord is with you.
Do not be afraid,
you have found favor with God.

I have made you
full with God's fruitfulness.
In the beginning I gave you this child
that waits for your precious will,
the love of your yes
that waits with the Word in paradise.

From your virgin life—
the creation of the virgin world.
You shall bear the beginning,
the command of creation
that is the source and the reason for your will
and yet waits for your yes.

The Holy Spirit will cloak you;
the power of the Most High will overshadow you.
The obscured presence, the veil to be torn,
the column of revelation, I Am in my temple.
An eternal kingship lives within you.

You will conceive in your womb and bear a son
who will be called the Son of God,
the Son of the Most High.
And God will give him a kingdom without end.
Nothing is impossible for God.

Behold
the revelation of the mystery
veiled for long ages
now manifest,
according to the command of the eternal God,
as promised by the prophets.

Behold
the purpose of life,
O my precious love,
I Am coming now,
and I Am coming always.

Announce
the birth of all,
the new heavens and the new earth,
the Almighty Word from which all springs,
existence and identity,
the command that brings life and spirit
from nothing.
This greeting
is the light that split the darkness on the first day.

Bear my truth.
Bear the Word coming into the world.
Whoever confesses the Son has the Father.
Let the Word you heard from the beginning
remain in you,
and you will remain in the Son and in the Father,
in my promise of eternal life.

The Lord adorns the lowly in victory.
The victor of the world is the one
who brings the Messiah into the world.

Sing a new song to the Lord.
Announce His salvation day after day.
Let the heavens and the earth be happy.
Let the seas and plains resound.
Let the rivers clap their hands.
And mountains and forests shout.

The Lord comes to rule the earth.
He comes to rule with justice.

You shall name the child Jesus,
because He shall save people from their sins.
At the name of Jesus every knee shall bend
on earth and below the earth.

Behold I am
the handmaid of the Lord.
May it be done to me according to your Word.

CONCEPTION BY THE HOLY SPIRIT

And the Word became flesh.

And dwells among us.
We see the glory of the Father's only Son,
Full of Grace, and truth.

The only Son reveals the Father.
I Am the way the truth and the life.
The divine will that enlightens.
See me and know yourself.

A sword pierces my heart.
A hand that wants to believe enters my wounds.
When it draws out,
it seems to draw out my heart also,
leaving me waiting to be filled by God.

Aflame with God's love,
the pain of my heart is so beautiful,
my sacred and immaculate heart.
So surpassing is the sweetness,
my suffering,
a caress of love between my soul and God.
My soul is satisfied with nothing less.

From this first moment,
when my will and flesh are one,
when the divine and human are joined,
I Am in a first tiny cell,
in my creation,
willed so vulnerable and so incarnate.

From this first moment
springs the conception of all flesh,
all agony in the void
and the abyss before the Word.
Springs paradise and will
and the wait for my glory.
Springs forever the majesty of my creative Word
who gives life freely and bears eternity.

Just as the heavens send the rain and snow
to make the world fertile and fruitful,
so shall my Word be.
The divine will goes forth from my mouth
and shall not return to me void,
but shall achieve the end for which I sent it.

I receive the flesh of God; the beginning of life.
I remain in Him; He remains in me,
in His Church, His body, His eternal.

Behold I Am with you always
even until the end of the world.

Your fidelity is undying, Lord.
Let your love enter me.

I Am love.
Whoever does not love remains in death.
Whoever is without love does not know me.

We love you, Lord, who first loved us.
If we love one another, you remain in us,
and your love is brought to perfection in us.
Whoever remains in love remains in God
and God in him.

Fear not, you who bear my love.
You shall not be put to shame.
You believe you have been in the desert
a long time,
but it has been a brief moment.
With tenderness
I take my creation back.

My love will never leave you.
My covenant will never be shaken.

My soul proclaims the greatness of the Lord,
and my spirit rejoices in God my savior.
The Mighty One has done great things for me.
His mercy is eternal and upon those who fear him.

He lifts up the lowly.
He scatters the proud.
He throws down rulers from their thrones.
He fills the hungry.
He does not forsake His promise.
He will not forsake us.

THE VISITATION

Blessed are you among women,
and blessed the fruit of your womb.
Blessed are you who believed
that what the Lord spoke would be fulfilled.

Visit me, Holy Mother, with your Word of truth.
Mary, with child by the Holy Spirit,
how is it that the Mother of my God comes to me?

How is it that the Ark comes to me?
The Covenant, God-Bearer,
where the Almighty resides
in the new temple He has ordained.

We leap and dance with all our might
before the Ark.
You carry the history of creation in your womb,
your flesh, the new altar of sacrifice.
You carry the undying hope
of all generations past who called to God.

Mother of the Church, come to us.
Chalice bearing eternal kingship,
the salvific blood of Messiah,
the eternal sacrament of the flesh,
visit us.

How is it, my incarnate God,
that you are what you have made,
that you have come to my poor flesh?

My old body is filled with sunsets.
All my hard triumphs are fleeting as days.
I am so afraid to close my eyes.
My bones are tired.
My mind is breathless
with meager stories and old promises.
Now I want only to kiss you, my precious life.

I was barren in the desert,
when I learned of my own fruitfulness,
when I learned of the coming child
who would make the way for God.
I wept to find a new eternity inside me.

A voice that cries out in the wilderness.
And even the mute for unbelief
cry out at the miraculous birth.

The unopened prophet's mouth
that lives in our dreams and promise
stirs to feel your magnificence close.
What is hidden from the wise and the learned
God has revealed to little children.
Out of the mouths of infants
God brings forth perfect praise.

And all the world
that has wailed for God
and cried out in barren wilderness
before memory,
all the world that lies waiting in its womb
leaps with joy.

TRAVEL TO BETHLEHEM AND REFUSAL AT THE INN

A decree went out from Caesar
that the whole world should be enrolled,
to count the souls each worth more than empires.

Those bringing God into the world
went to be counted among the world,
Joseph with Mary, his betrothed, with child.
They returned to Bethlehem,
the city and house of David.

The Word came to what was His own,
but His own did not know Him.
The Son of Man has nowhere to lay His head.

In the pregnant night,
in the anticipation of God,
with the Messiah fulfilled in Mary's womb,
who will invite them in?

Do not let your hearts be troubled.
The house of my Father has many rooms.
I Am preparing a place for you,
and I will come back again and take you to myself,
so where I Am you may also be.
Where I Am going you know the way.

I Am the way
the truth and the light.
No one comes to the Father except through me.
And through me all may come.
My house is a house of prayer for all peoples.

Father,
happy are those who live in your house.
Beautiful is your dwelling place,
every place where your life is.
My heart and my flesh where I dwell
cry out for the living God.

Trust in the Lord forever.
The lofty city He brings down.
He humbles it to the ground,
levels it with the dust.
It is trampled underfoot by the needy,
trampled beneath the footsteps of the poor.

My kingdom is not of this world
that refuses the gift of its own life.
I will purify the mouths of the peoples
so they may call upon my name
and serve me with one accord.
You belong to me, not to the world.

And on that day you need not be ashamed.
As we were in paradise,
you will be transformed.

Unashamed, the Holy Family
made their place around a manger.
And Holy God, Mighty One, Eternal One,
waited among the lowly of creation,
the work of His own hands,
and saw that it was very good.

VISION OF THE MAGI

We see your light.
We are coming to you where we belong.
The glories of the world point all and only to you,
and we follow.
We are nothing without this search
to kneel before almighty truth.

Where is the newborn king,
the ruler who is to shepherd His people?
We saw His star at its rising,
and we come to do Him homage.

We are coming and all the world is coming:
children first,
women and men,
all peoples,
all persons,
all races,
all creeds.

All broken hopes,
the weak and the strong of spirit,
the poor and the poor of heart,
the simple and the lost,
the saints and the clouded.

Believers and non-believers,
the joyous and the desolate,
the fruitful and the barren,
and even we who wish to sing your Word
from our clods of river and clay.

Of all those who come,
the servants come first,
the lowly first and those who know betrayal.

We all struggle towards your star,
Lord, our only need.
We come despite our sin.
We hunger and thirst for righteousness.
Where else would we go?
You have the Word of life.

Nations walk by God's light.
Raise your eyes and look about,
the people of the world come to God's promise.
You shall be radiant at what you see.
You heart shall throb and overflow.

The Father has raised up for us a mighty Savior.
He has come to his people and set them free.
In the tender compassion of our God
the dawn from on high breaks upon us,
to shine on those who dwell in darkness
and the shadow of death,
and guide our feet on the way of peace.

Justice flowers in the Messiah.
He rescues the poor who cry out
and the afflicted who have no one to help them.
He pities the lowly and saves the lives of the poor.
His name will be blessed forever.

I Am coming to you now,
and I Am coming always.
As I Am the beginning,
I Am also the end.

As all nations come to me,
all nations should expect to see my glory.
The one true child king you seek.
I gather what is mine to myself.

We who search unendingly
share our joy at finding you,
to the ends of the earth and its jealous princes.

I too wish to do Him homage,
says the liar.
And the liar sees the same glory.

THE VIRGIN GIVES BIRTH TO GOD IN A STABLE

The way of the Lord dilates my heart.
Gates lift up your heads.
Stand erect ancient doors
and let in the king of glory.

We who walked in darkness
have seen a great light.
We rejoice as at the harvest,
because God has smashed our oppression
and overcome our famine.

A child is born to us.
A son is given to us who is Messiah.
Upon His shoulder dominion rests,
and rests the weight of the world.
God the Mighty, Father-Forever,
Prince of Peace.

We have seen our creation,
our salvation, and our selves.
Who has seen the Son has seen the Father.

Let the earth exult and bear fruit.
Let the ends of the earth give thanks
and stand in awe that God is just.
My poor clay does not know
how to be grateful enough for the gift of life.

In the fullness of time,
God sent His only Son born of a woman
to ransom captive creation.
To make us God's children.

Behold the Father's justice:
this is my beloved Son,
body, blood, soul, and divinity.

Behold the flesh created by God:
the flesh of paradise,
the resurrection of the body.

Behold the power of God:
that He may be so vulnerable,
even as an infant.
This is the love that makes us His own.
The peace that surpasses all understanding.

I bear up the weakness of humanity.
I know every temptation of the flesh.
I come humbly before I come in glory.
I Am where you are.
There is no place where I Am not.

He is born with every outcast.
Born with every exile.
Born with the abandoned.

Mary wrapped him in swaddling clothes
and laid him in a manger,
while the world hungers only for Him,
lives only for Him and because of Him.
His infant sigh fills our lungs
and enkindles in us the fire of His love.

Be not afraid.
God goes before us always.
From the womb He goes first in our flesh
to open the desert,
and with joy we draw water
from the fountain of salvation:

I Am one with your flesh.
To do my will from the beginning,
I put my Spirit in you.
Behold the infant cause of life
and give your lives to me.
Behold, uplifted, the dawn of new time.

I do not desire the offerings of the past.
I created all things, they belong to me.
I gave you the law to preserve you in wait,
but now you have seen the final temple of God.

Now I desire your will, your love.
These are all you can give me,
all else is mine.

I give you your freedom,
so you have love to return.
Rend your hearts,
as I open my sacred heart of flesh.
What you do to the least, you do to me.

I give you my Son, to see my face in your own.
I give you His sacrifice,
for you to return to me in atonement.
I give you again the flesh of the beginning.
My Word's obedience is your breath.
You have born all history for this first truth.

There will be signs in the sky and stars.
Nations will be in dismay.
People will die in anticipation of what comes.
The powers of Heaven will be shaken.

And you will see the Son of Man
seated at the right hand of the Power
and coming on the clouds of Heaven.
Stand erect and raise your heads.
Your redemption is at hand.

PROCLAMATION
TO THE SHEPHERDS

Shepherds kept watch over their flocks at night,
to see that not one sheep was lost,
when the glory of the Lord shone around them,
and they were struck with fear.

Do not be afraid.
I proclaim good news of great joy
for all people.

Today a savior is born for you.
He is Messiah and Lord.

I Am the Good Shepherd.
I walk ahead of my sheep through the darkness.
I know them and they know me,
and they recognize my voice.

I came so you might have life
and have it more abundantly.
I Am the gate to paradise.
Whoever enters through me will be saved.
I lay down in the gate to the pasture.
I do not flee from the wolves.

I Am the Good Shepherd
that lays down His life for His sheep.
No one takes my life from me;
I lay it down on my own.
I have power to lay it down and take it up again.

The Lord is my shepherd,
I shall not want.
He gives me peace in His beauty.
He refreshes my soul.

He guides me in right paths,
to be glorious by saving me.
I fear no evil,
He is at my side.
He has gone before me,
He gives me courage.

Do you love me?
Yes, Lord. I love you.
Feed my lambs.

Do you love me?
Yes, Lord. I love you.
Tend my sheep.

Do you love me?
Lord, you know all things.
You know that I love you.
Feed my sheep.

If you have ears you should hear:
I Am teaching you shepherds to love.
I Am giving you the fullness of humanity,
who goes before you into tribulation,
who goes before you into the night,
into the void,
to tear it in two with the light of life.
I reside creating where you see emptiness.

You are the shepherds in care of the weak,
in care of souls, I trust you to one another.
I trust you with myself.
You who go after one lost sheep
and rejoice when it is found.
Take up the selfless life that I give,
and by your labor glorify my kingdom.

Do not break upon your loneliness.
Do not break upon the impossible
beauty of your hope.
I shepherd you to life
beyond what you can know.

Behold I Am coming to you.
I Am coming now,
and I Am coming always.
Hear my voice and follow me.

You will find the cause of all creation,
an infant wrapped in swaddling clothes
and lying in a manger.

EPIPHANY

Shepherds glorify what angels proclaimed.
Kings kneel bearing gifts
of kingship, priesthood, and sacrament.
The prophetic star proceeds all
to the place where the infant lay.

Our life fulfilled,
the flesh of God,
we receive incarnate
the mystery of the beginning.
It is as though God has just now breathed
in my lungs of clay.

The world sees Him as He is and gives homage,
a universal Eucharist
that creates and sustains the world.
Rejoice, ruins of Jerusalem.

The ends of the earth behold
our God to whom we look to save us,
for whom we waited through virgin ages.
The throne of God descends,
hewn in our poor flesh.
Make us turn to you;
if only we see your face or touch you
we shall be healed.

Among your ruins I make my throne.
I know your every suffering.
I shall be an infant
so not to overwhelm you with my glory,
and to be gloriously unbound.
I shall be humble as bread
so not to destroy you.
To love me, choose me in faith.

Messiah, you make our flesh and our will
your temple and your eternal sacrifice,
the sacred place of your transfiguration.
The Kingdom of God is within us.

All nations stream toward God's highest mountain,
God's temple, where God will provide.
He destroys the veil that conceals us.
He destroys death forever.
He wipes the tears from our faces,
He has spoken His Word.

I live upon His mountain,
and I am His mountain,
where they brought the sick and lame,
the blind and mute, and many others.
They laid them at His feet, and he healed them.

Out of the gloom and darkness
the eyes of the blind see,
the hungry tyrant shall be no more,
and the hungry abyss is filled.
From a few loaves and fishes He fed them.

All who are thirsty, come and drink.
All who have no money, come and eat.
Come without paying and without cost.
Why spend your wages for what is not bread,
for what fails to satisfy?

Put on the splendor of the glory of God forever.
Fill your mouth with laughter.
Those who go out weeping, carrying the seed,
will come back rejoicing carrying the harvest.

See in the Virgin's arms the seed of life.
Through the Son, I make you my own children.
When you were woven in the depths of the earth
I saw you in the womb.
Even darkness is not dark to me.
To me light and dark are the same.

The seed grows, the Word in us.
We do not belong to the world but to God.
See what love the Father has bestowed on us
that we may be called His children.

Behold the first fruits and see your infant self.
We are God's children now.
What we shall be is a mystery.
When it is revealed we shall be like Him,
for we shall see Him as He is.

The darkness is passing away,
and the true light is already shining.

FLIGHT TO EGYPT AND
MURDER OF THE INNOCENTS

In Joseph's second dream the Lord said: Rise,
Take the child and his mother, and flee to Egypt.
Herod will search for the child to destroy Him.

As the Holy Family fled by night
the ancient path of God's salvation,
the king cried out in his palace:
there is a living seed.
I sow a thousand seeds of chaos and destruction,
and choke on what we reap.

But the Magi humbled themselves
before the source of their kingship,
and protected the child from Herod.
And Herod could not see the child.
And Herod did not know the child.

I am afraid of the coming of the promised king.
I am afraid that He will take away my own power.
I am afraid of His love.
I am afraid of His commands.
I want no sovereign in my selfish kingdom.

Order the death of all boys in Bethlehem
two years old and under.

And the city wept for its children,
and the people cried out like the exile.
They mourned the tyranny of death,
their weeping heard through the countryside.

There was no consolation
when there was no child.

There is no king but God,
merciful and gracious,
slow to anger and abounding in kindness,
who forgives our sins and heals our ills.
He redeems life from true destruction
and crowns us with compassion.

The innocent die
only in the eyes of the foolish world.
They tread the path of God's own hallowed name,
God's own power and glory.
It is the pure victims that have subdued the world
that is powerless against their eternity.

The gates of hell
will not prevail against the Church.
The way of the wicked vanishes,
and their memory perishes,
and their lawless deeds convict them to their face.

But the Lord guides the way of the just.
He stretches out the heavens like a veil
to dwell in His temple beneath them.

To Him, the nations are as dust.
He makes kings and brings princes to naught.
He makes the rulers of the earth as nothing.
Their stem is rooted in the earth.
He breathes upon them, and they wither.
The storm carries them away.

But he gives strength to the faint.
He exults his temple.
He renews those with faith,
they soar to Him like eagles,
and their love flourishes in His glory.
They persist and do not grow weary.

RETURN OUT OF EGYPT

Out of Egypt I called my Son.
Joseph learned in his third dream:
Those who sought the child's life are dead.

The Holy Family
makes their way through the vast desert.
Our waiting voices cry out of the wilderness:
make straight the way of the Lord.

He comes in the flesh
along the ancient path of exodus,
to break the chains of sin and death.

He goes toward the mountain,
to make the new law,
to transform our human flesh
in a command of selfless love,
one life with all salvation's wait.

He is the covenant with all creation,
the promise in our hearts' first beating,
the command of life,
the breath of God,
the Word spoke even at the moment of the fall.

He is the covenant of the flood,
and He is the high waters.
By man shall blood be shed,
for in the image of God has man been made.
He gives us the only sacrifice
worthy of return to Him.

He is a child of Abraham and abides by the law.
The son and the lamb upon the altar,
presented in the Temple after forty days
and consecrated to the Father,
when Mary sacrifices two doves
because she cannot afford a lamb.

He bears our forty years in the wandering desert,
when He goes into the wilderness
where we cannot bear the wait,
to be tempted three times with our world.

He is transfigured on mountaintops,
faced with the decree of the Father.

The final prophet sees His power
to raise children from the stones,
who knows the imminence of heaven
and that the fruitless will be cut down,
who will preach a man coming after
who ranks ahead because he existed before.

He is baptized,
the first in the final covenant,
when the sky is torn open,
the world is flooded with God's Word,
and alights Noah's still searching dove.
He gathers fishers of men
to draw us up from the baptism.

He is sacramental Israel,
revelation and the fullness of time.
He returns from the beginning
to gather all people to himself;
to gather His Church and His body;
to go to the depths of death to gather the lost.
He subjugates all to the will of creation.

It is our flesh a sword will pierce,
as the transfigured flesh of the Messiah,
as the martyrs of the Church that is His body.
Place your hand in the wound of my side
and do not be unbelieving but believe.

Vulnerable as an infant but with almighty power,
ever-present, in the temple of our transfigured flesh,
His eternity is upon our tongue.
We can die in peace
because our eyes have seen your salvation,
the revelation and glory of all people.

The Holy Family approaches from the desert,
the final exodus
when the infant Messiah leads all
toward the new creation and the new covenant.

The child king that wears creation as His raiment,
as He would wear the sky and all the stars,
as He wears the supreme beauty
of ever-spilling life.

Alpha and omega.
First and last.
With His beginning He brings the end.

Have we the strength to ask for His coming?
We ask, at last, for justice.
But I fear that you are just.
We lift up our hearts to your mercy,
but my heart shames me.
Can we mean what we pray?

Ask or do not ask.
I Am coming now,
and I Am coming always,
to create a new heaven and a new earth.
The end comes like a thief in the night.

The Holy Family approaches from the desert;
prepare the way of the Lord.
Every valley shall be filled,
every mountain made low.

The glory of the Lord shall be revealed.
We shall see it together.

Go onto a high mountain,
while the mountain exists,
and cry out at the top of your voice.
Fear not to cry out,
and say here is your God.
Here He comes with power,
gathering us into His arms.
Whoever has ears ought to hear.

We are dying.
Dying with pain for paradise.
We are nothing but the loving want for you, Messiah.
We are in labor,
bringing birth to our names in the dust and ash.
Do not let the temple of my poor heart fail.
Do not let me go down into the dust.

Give us new life and we will call upon your name.
You sent the spirit of your Son into our hearts,
crying out Father, Father.
Open my lips
and my mouth will proclaim your praise.
You put this need in me.
Do not leave it unsatisfied.

In the beginning you created me,
throughout all ages destined to exist.
I want your font.
I want your truth.
I want the courage to bear fruit
in the shortness of days.
Speak the Word and command us to life.
Let the earth open up and salvation bud forth.

I have created this earth to bear fruit,
created you to glorify my life that you are.
I made you to love you
and to be one with my love.
You were in me when
I laid the world's foundations.

I Am Who Is, there is no other.
To me every knee shall bend.
I Am the vindication and the glory.
I Am the incorruptible fountain.
I Am the resurrection and the life.
I Am coming with power on the clouds of heaven,

The world of the past is gone.
Behold, I make all creation new.
You bring to me the altar of the flesh for healing:
I Am who made your flesh the altar.
Be it done unto you according to your faith.

Be it done unto me according to your Word.

Open your ears and hear,
and rise up out of sleep to life.
With my Word, with this flesh,
I open forever the gates of paradise.
The eternal Kingdom of Heaven is at hand.

Ephatha!
Ephatha!
Ephatha!